VAN GOGH

Van Gogh

BY RENÉ HUYGHE

CROWN PUBLISHERS, INC. - NEW YORK

Title page: SELF-PORTRAIT, 1887
Oil on canvas, 19″ × 15″ (48.3 × 38 cm)
Rijksmuseum Vincent van Gogh, Amsterdam

Translated from the French by:
HELEN C. SLONIM

Series published under the direction of:
MADELEINE LEDIVELEC-GLOECKNER

Library of Congress Cataloging in Publication Data

Huyghe, René.
Van Gogh.

(Crown art library)
1. Gogh, Vincent van, 1853-1890 — Criticism and interpretation.   2. Painting, Dutch.   3. Painting, Modern — 19th century — Netherlands.   I. Title.
II. Series.
ND653.G7H93   1988   759.9492   88-445
ISBN 0-517-00500-X

PRINTED IN ITALY – INDUSTRIE GRAFICHE CATTANEO S.P.A., BERGAMO
© 1977 BONFINI PRESS CORPORATION, NAEFELS, SWITZERLAND
REVISED EDITION

We are awed before we even start writing about Van Gogh. It is not of a painter, but of a soul, that we are about to speak. This is the story of a soul fighting against the supreme problems of destiny. Van Gogh lived these problems in the core of the tragedy which makes the modern world — our tragedy — with its outbursts, its unlimited yearning, its failures, its desperation. However present, however much a symbol of our times, his work cannot be considered only, in its paroxysm, as an image of contemporary soul; it also unveils, in its deepest expression, the soul of eternal man. Few writers, few artists, have felt and expressed, as Van Gogh did, the pathetic situation of human condition.

This tragedy, into which he threw himself until he could but die, is the tragedy of going beyond, the tragedy of the absolute which burns out the purest and most exacting souls. They all suffer from man's duality; man hanging, torn, between two poles. One still in contact with the beast, the other already reaching up to God. This is man's unsolvable paradox. Being of the flesh, he is deeply etched in the physical world and its sorrows; he bears the brand of all that is matter; he is an accident which happened in space and time, accidentally appearing in a universe which he does not understand but which he suffers; his fate is to disappear with the second which carries him; decay is his only short reprieve from nothingness. But man is also a being of the soul and, as such, has a yearning for the absolute; if he can neither achieve it nor live it, he can at least conceive it and be obsessed by it. He perceives a conscience of which he is only the

In the Church, 1882.   Watercolor, 11″ × 15″ (27 × 37).   Private collection

Portrait of a Woman half-length, 1883
Pencil and ink wash
15½" × 10" (39 × 24.5 cm)
Rijksmuseum Vincent van Gogh
Amsterdam

Woman's Head, 1881-1883
Pen and ink, 8½" × 5" (21 × 13 cm)
Private collection

7

Man Praying, 1883
Black pencil and India ink
22½″ × 18½″ (56 × 46 cm)
Private collection

Peasant Mowing, 1885
Black pencil, 16½″ × 20½″ (41 × 51 cm)
Rijksmuseum Vincent van Gogh
Amsterdam

THE POTATO EATERS, 1885
Oil on canvas, 32¼″ × 45″ (82 × 114 cm)
Rijksmuseum Vincent van Gogh
Amsterdam

Man with Top Hat, 1882
Pencil
17½″ × 10″ (43.5 × 24 cm)
Private collection

Old Man with Top Hat, 1882
Black pencil, ink and wash
24″ × 14½″ (60.5 × 36 cm)
Rijksmuseum Vincent van Gogh
Amsterdam

infinitely small and caricatural image, which would break loose from the particular, from the transitory, from the uncertain. He calls it God. There he lies, miserable and awed, between abjection and glory. Different from all other living creatures of this world, he is conscious of this abjection and cannot stand it; he is conscious of this glory and cannot reach it. He

THE WEAVER, 1884
Watercolor, 14″ × 10″ (35 × 25 cm)
Rijksmuseum Vincent van Gogh
Amsterdam

HEAD OF A PEASANT WOMAN, 1885
Oil on canvas mounted on wood, 16⅛″ × 12⅜″ (41 × 31.5 cm).   Private collection

Sorrow, 1882
Lithograph, 18″ × 12″ (46 × 30.5 cm)

Peasant Woman Bending Over, 1885
Black pencil, 21" × 17" (52 × 43 cm)
Rijksmuseum Kröller-Müller, Otterlo

common. The hope of each is multiplied by the hope of every one; a religion is born. Then, sometimes they are alone, they move forward leaning on their feeble strength with doubt and misgiving. If they write, they incessantly scan their own minds; if they paint, they incessantly scan their own faces, for they know that only in themselves will they find the opening of a clear path. And often, their fellowmen are frightened away and only come back later to worship their remains and their traces. This was Van Gogh's destiny.

Peasant Woman Gleaning, 1883-1885
Black pencil, 21" × 17" (52 × 43 cm)
Private collection

understands what he would like to be and cannot understand what he actually is. His only reaction facing this unsolvable contradiction is a total numbness or a moral tearing apart and accompanying cries.

Van Gogh uttered one of the most violent of these cries, one of the most tragic, one of those "passionate sobs," mentioned by Charles Baudelaire who considered them "the most certain evidence we can give of our dignity." Sometimes, with this incentive, with a desire to free themselves and go beyond themselves, men set off in

14

Studies for a Nude Child, Sitting, 1885-1886.   Black pencil, 19″ × 12½″ (47.5 × 31 cm)
Rijksmuseum Vincent van Gogh, Amsterdam

By the end of this 19th century which finally completed the failure of common convictions and left to his individual loneliness any man concerned about his fate and his reason for living, Van Gogh, man of passion and turmoil, could only live his venture by separating himself from the others and sinking into himself. Driven by his instinctive power, pushed by anguish, overriding his panic and his doubt by fierce and angry eyes in a bony and hairy face — he was more than a painter expressing the terrible image of his soul; he was a mind, seeking his dreadful way with acts and words, with passion and nobility.   His painting, which seems to flow from him, almost instinctive in its irresistible violence, was his last resort.   It took him many a distressing experience before he realized that only when holding a paint-brush could he find, or hope to find, a way.   And as he fought with words he struggled with pictures!   He is one of those artists whose writings should be dipped into at all times.   His letters deserve a place beside

JAPONAISERIE: THE FLOWERING
PLUM TREES (AFTER HIROSHIGE), 1887
Oil on canvas, 21¾″ × 18″ (55 × 46 cm)
Rijksmuseum Vincent van Gogh, Amsterdam

PORTRAIT OF PÈRE TANGUY, 1887
Oil on canvas
21⅝″ × 20⅛″ (65 × 51 cm)
Private collection

16

Le Père Tanguy, 1887
Pencil, 8½" × 5" (21.5 × 13.5 cm)
Rijksmuseum Vincent van Gogh
Amsterdam

the "Diary" of Eugène Delacroix. Their style may not be correct, first because any means of expression was a battle for him, but also because this Dutchman lived in France, used French most of the time, and his normally entangled speech was still complicated by handling foreign words, belatedly learned. But this clumsiness itself gives a harsher and more heart-gripping tone to his questioning voice.

In his letters — the most beautiful and most significant were addressed to his brother Theo who helped him all along his brief existence — he asks himself: "I always have the impression of being a traveler going somewhere, to some destination. If I say to myself: This somewhere, this destination does not exist, it seems to me to be true and well-reasoned. And at the end of my career I will be in the wrong: I will then find out that not only the fine arts, but even the rest were nothing but dreams and that one's self was nothing at all."

Is life, then, definitely incomprehensible? Is there no glimmer in all this darkness? "So and so does not always know himself what he could do, but by instinct he feels: I am good at something. I feel there is a reason for my being alive..." There lies the way: "My torture is nothing more than this: In what way could I be good for something! Couldn't I help, be useful for something?" Not to know what to do, how to do it, nor what to expect from one's self! "I know that I could be an utterly different man. There is something inside me. What can it be?"

Self-Portrait with Gray Felt Hat, 1887.   Oil on canvas, 17¼″ × 14¾″ (44 × 37.5 cm)
Rijksmuseum Vincent van Gogh, Amsterdam

Nude, ca 1887
Pencil, 10″ × 12½″ (24 × 31 cm)
Rijksmuseum Vincent van Gogh
Amsterdam

NUDE WOMAN RECLINING, 1887
Oil on canvas
9½″ × 16¼″ (24 × 41 cm)
Private colletion

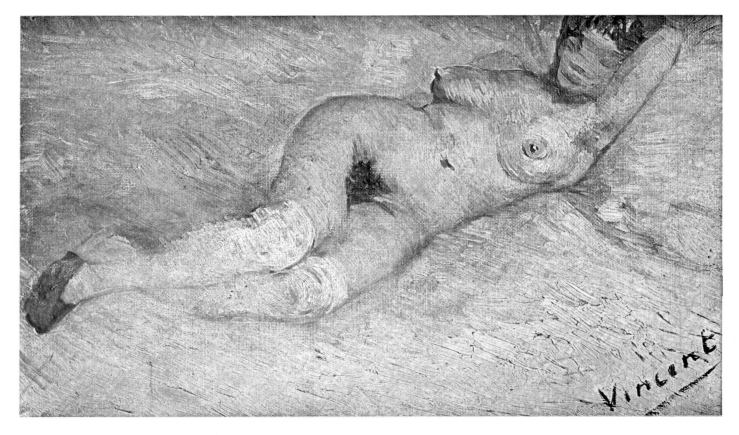

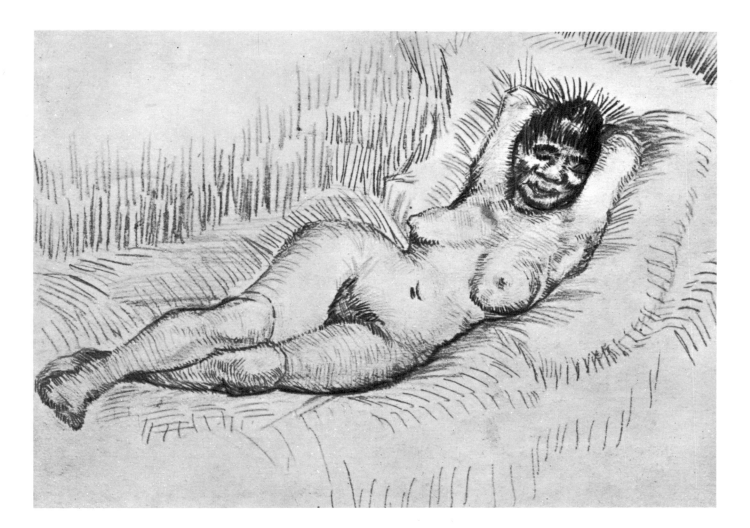

But is an act of faith enough? Yearning is no answer, it is only the desire of an answer. Before yielding to the answer, one must find it. So, this being, who is absolutely sincere, who is not satisfied with mere sentences or fine words, who seeks like a blind man feeling his way with his fingers, but can then grasp what he finds, plunges his searching hands into the depths of himself. And what he first meets is something vague: a warmth. "I feel in myself a fire which I cannot let die out; on the contrary I must quicken it, although I don't know where this will lead me." His mind still does not know that toward which he is going, but he perceives a faint glimmer. He goes toward it and discovers a fire burning deep within himself, and this is already a certainty. There is a fire, and this fire must be used for something. It is not enough to have found it, it is not even enough to be burned out by it, this fire must have some sort of use; the problem is still there and he must start groping again to find another way. "It is like a great blaze in your soul, and nobody ever comes to warm himself by it. The passers-by just see a little smoke, there at the top, coming out of the chimmey, and walk on. Now the question is, what to do?"

Is it enough to be and to wait? "Keep this fire burning inside yourself, sense your own value, and yet wait patiently — oh how impatiently — wait, say I, for the time when somebody, anybody, will come and sit by the fire, will stay there, or do something?" How significant is this mental image of a fire! It burns his mind and bursts out in his pictures. If — as Marcel Proust believed — each artist, each writer, can be summed up by a symbolical image, or even — according to Gaston Bachelard — by an "element" corresponding to his inner nature, Van Gogh can without doubt be interpreted by fire. In this, he brings to the mind another great Dutch painter, Rembrandt. But the latter saw the fire as a central brightness which pushed aside the heavy burden of darkness and where he could light the warm radiance of kindness. Van Gogh's fire is more terrible, more spasmodic, more consuming. It destroys as well as it quickens; it can be a sign of death as well as a sign of life.

Its flame dances; now it jumps up in a great blaze, now it fades and seems ready to go out. Then, Van Gogh loses again the brightness he was following: "What good can I be, he kept asking, what can I be useful for? There is something inside me. What, but what is it? ...Men are often prevented from doing anything, prisoners of I don't know what horrible, horrible, most horrible cage!" From his pen flow out words which are almost Shakespeare's. "One cannot always say what shuts you in, walls you in, seems to bury you, but one feels nevertheless, I don't know what bars, what gates, what walls... and then one asks: My God, is it for long, is it for ever, is it for eternity?" And thus goes on and on, in an unrelenting circle, the round of the prisoners, at the bottom of the dark pit which is their yard, enclosed on all sides by doorless walls. It is known that he painted this prisoners' walk under the shock he experienced on seeing a drawing of Gustave Doré, and one can guess the deep meaning which he immediately gave it: "This something which is called *the soul*, one claims it never dies and always lives — and seeks always, always, and again and always!" (see page 69).

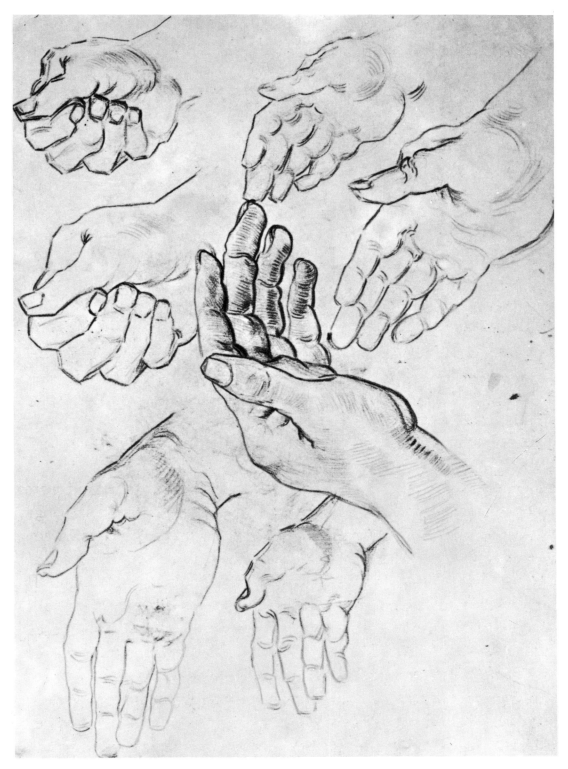

Study Sheet with Seven Hands, 1886-1888.   Black pencil, 13″ × 10″ (32 × 24 cm)
Rijksmuseum Vincent van Gogh, Amsterdam

La Guinguette, 1887
Pen and pencil, 15″ × 20″ (37.5 × 50 cm)
Rijksmuseum Vincent van Gogh, Amsterdam

ALMOND TREE IN BLOSSOM, 1888
Oil on canvas, 19¾″ × 15″ (50,5 × 38 cm)
Rijksmuseum Vincent van Gogh, Amsterdam

THE LANGLOIS BRIDGE WITH
WOMEN WASHING, 1888
Oil on canvas, 21¼″ × 25½″ (54 × 65 cm)
Rijksmuseum Kröller-Müller, Otterlo

Boats at Saintes-Maries, 1888
Black pencil
16″ × 21½″ (39.5 × 53.5 cm)
Private collection

Bridge on the Rhône, 1888
Reed pen, 10″ × 10½″ (24.3 × 31.6 cm)
Private collection

Quay with Men Unloading Sand Barges, 1888
Oil on canvas, 21⅝″ × 28″ (55 × 66 cm)
Museum Folkwang, Essen

Sᴜɴꜰʟᴏᴡᴇʀꜱ, 1887.   Oil on canvas, 23⅝″ × 39⅜″ (60 × 100 cm)
Rijksmuseum Kröller-Müller, Otterlo

First one must want and persist. "Where there is a will, there is a way." "Even if I fall ninety-nine times, the hundredth I will get up once again." The circle turns and endlessly starts the same course over again. Why should it break? It is bound and limited by high walls. Thus reasons whoever only looks at his own level and straight ahead. But in the opening over and above the prisoners' walk a small patch of sky can be seen. Maybe it is enough to look above oneself? "You need something big, something infinite where you can *see God.*"

Garden with Sunflowers, 1888
Pencil and reed pen
23⅞" × 19⅛" (60.5 × 48.7 cm)
Rijksmuseum Vincent van Gogh
Amsterdam

And just as Van Gogh found the fire, following Rembrandt's footsteps, he also discovered, like Rembrandt, what feeds it and makes it shoot forth up to that little opening high above. Fire, by its human name, is called love. And Van Gogh is perhaps the only painter, with Rembrandt, who based his whole art on love. He knows now how to call this blaze: It is the fire of love, the "fuego amoroso" which Saint John of the Cross had already revealed.

"Involuntarily, I always think that the best way of knowing God, is to love a great deal!" "It is good to love as much as one can, for there is the real strength, and one who loves a great deal achieves great things and is capable of it, and what is done through love is well done."

During this too short life, Van Gogh will have the time to find out that good will and even love can go amiss. He will fall on his knees several times; he will get up again, without surrendering. He will then discover the meaning and the requirements of this fire and this love which are devouring him: "I cannot do without something which is greater than I, which is my whole life: the power

Roulin the Postman, 1888
Reed pen, 13″ × 10″ (31.8 × 24.3 cm)
Private collection

to create". The day he made this discovery, he became a painter. But he still will have to discover, painfully, what is his painting, his real painting, the one he was made to paint. And at that time, he will have about three more years to live...

This is the story that should now be told. Vincent van Gogh was born on the 30th of March, 1853, in Holland, at Groot-Zundert, in Northern Brabant. He is a Northerner. He does not come from those Latin countries where thought is the basis of harmony and equilibrium, organizing and regulating. Of course, a man from the North is usually practical. But as soon as thought starts seething in him, it adds a halo of uneasiness and perturbation to reality; it pushes reality away from any secure connection: the concrete. The man drifts away into the imaginary, he breaks the circle of security. Thus starts the adventure of the unknown. He becomes a man possessed by the soul.

Furthermore, Van Gogh is a Protestant, a son and grandson of ministers, that is he comes from a religion whose straightness will not allow soft-hearted hesitations. Let this sensitivity and feelings get loose and they will also burn and destroy. Rembrandt too, was a Protestant, but he could not have said, as Van Gogh did in 1877: "As far back as one can remember there was always a servant of the Gospel in our family, from generation to generation."

Nevertheless he seeks his way in another direction. Like a premonition of his later destiny, but misdirected, he is attracted by art. Of his three uncles, two were art dealers. His idea is to do the same thing. One of his uncles, who owned an art gallery in The Hague, had sold it to Goupil who was at that time owner of one of the main art galleries in Paris.   On July 30, 1869, the Goupil Gallery in The Hague hires Vincent as salesman.   He is soon sent to their gallery in Brussels and in May, 1873 to the London branch.   There, the young man, who despite his middle-class upbringing had been a somewhat hunted-looking youth, neglecting his appearance, aggressive and awkward, seems to accept the standards of life. Like so many young men, despite all his smouldering inside passions, he seems to submit himself to a regular way of living.   Like so many young men he is in love, in love with the first young girl he encounters.   She is the daughter of Van Gogh's landlady, her name is Ursule Loyer.   He asks her to marry him and is rejected.   He is in love, but he has not yet understood that love can only achieve its fullness through giving and not through greed.   This failure, his first failure, heavily affects his hypernervous and unsteady nature, he falls apart.   He leaves London, comes to Paris, goes back to London, and finally, in May 1875, manages to get work at the Goupil Gallery in Paris.

In this center of intellectual effervescence, he starts escaping the limitations of his job.   He visits the museums, grows enthusiastic at seeing the masterpieces, reads a lot, but as a man who is self-taught.   This is in 1875: The humanitarian idealism which soared up with the French revolution of 1848 has not yet seen its blazing generous illusions smolder down.   Van Gogh is gripped by Dostoievsky and Tolstoy.   While in England, his reading of George Eliot had somewhat prepared him for the Russian authors by setting his mind upon the sufferings of the humble. He finds this same accent of human generosity in Millet's paintings, and he will never cease to admire this artist.   And finally, heredity brings him to the Bible, which will become his fundamental reading.   And later on, the heavy volume, handed down from century to century, will take its place in his painting, as it had already been represented in many a painting of Rembrandt.

At that period a first mutation takes place: Van Gogh seems incapable of having normal social contacts; irritations, conflicts burst out and pile up.   Hardly a year goes by before Goupil dismisses him.   But his religious vocation is roused. He goes back to England and obtains a job as assistant teacher with a minister in Ramsgate.   Entrusted with collecting the pupils' boarding fees in a miserable and popular district, he accomplishes this task as badly as possible and loses his job.   He is again employed as teacher by a Methodist minister and becomes, to use his own words: "Something between a minister and a missionary."

His religious heredity's call and his feeling for the humble, inspire him to apply for a position as evangelist among the miners. "I feel attracted by religion. I want to comfort the humble." His request is not granted, because, so he is told, he is too young. So he goes back to Etten to spend Christmas 1876 with his parents.

Another commercial venture, as clerk in a bookshop in Dordrecht, does not last long. He believes he knows by now where his future lies: Religion is the opening he needs. But there too, good-will is not enough. He needs to expand his too superficial and hasty education. Therefore he prepares himself to enter the Theological Seminary in Amsterdam. But how could he possibly conform to collective and regular methods of education? With a nature as tumultuous as his, he realizes he will never succed. He comes back to his family to brood over this new failure. Then, in August 1878, he makes a decision, goes to a school in Brussels and three months later he is called (his dream come true) to the most outcast, the most tragically miserable part of Belgium: The mining country, the Borinage. He first goes to Pâturage, near Mons, then settles down in Wasmes. Feverishly he puts into action his idea of the pastorate. Impelled by his great feeling for poverty, he thinks the times of Saint Francis of Assisi, or the times of Christ are not so obsolete and that religion can be brought to the poor by putting oneself on the same level of destitution. He dresses like a miner; he lives in a wooden shack, sleeps on a pallet covered with pieces of old coats; he cuts out his puttees of coal sacks and, blackened with the mine's dust, he tries to lead the same life as the colliers and show them that he is one of them. It was with deep emotion that I held in my own hands the Bible of Van Gogh, the evangelist! It was loaned to me by a Swiss minister who had been fortunate enough to acquire it! Van Gogh had underlined in the margin the parts which impressed him most: The most dramatic, the most terrible, the most desperate (see page 5). Pharisees are of all times: Van Gogh's superiors do not appreciate his zeal. Like Saint Francis before him, Van Gogh causes a scandal. Very soon he is dismissed, no doubt politely and courteously, but definitely. He is told that he lacks perhaps the eloquence indispensable to his profession...

After the failure of individual love, which marked him so deeply when he was in England, he now has to face the failure of collective love, love of mankind by the Scriptures. There we may be touching the core of the crisis which Van

Café Terrace at Night, 1888.   Oil on canvas, 31⅞″ × 26″ (81 × 65.6 cm)
Rijksmuseum Kröller-Müller, Otterlo

La Mousmée, 1888. Oil on canvas, 28⅞″ × 23¾″ (73.3 × 60.3 cm)
National Gallery of Art, Washington D.C. Chester Dale Collection

THE ZOUAVE, 1888.   Oil on canvas, 31⅜″ × 25⅝″ (81 × 65 cm)
Private collection

Sitting Zouave, 1888
Pencil and reed pen, 19¼" × 24" (49 × 61 cm)
Rijksmuseum Vincent van Gogh, Amsterdam

Gogh lived and which we are still living. The crisis of our time is no doubt the crisis of individualism which cannot be solved simply — as some new form of civilisation proposes — by replacing it by collectivism. In a way, the birth of Protestantism is already the consequence of Western man's evolution toward individualism. But the latter, born at the end of the Middle Ages, received from the reformed religion a new stimulus which strongly helped its expression. Before that, man had formed the habit of only considering himself in connection with society; he could not imagine himself distinct from society. Thus, during the Middle Ages, it took very exceptional circumstances for an artist even to think of losing his anonymity and sign his own name to his works! He felt he was a good worker in a great collective effort which was the work of humanity in his time.

Since his beginning, had man ever ceased to exist within a social concept, expressed especially by religion? The first attempt to escape had been made by the Greeks who asked for the recognition and expansion of the individual, but that had sunk with the decadence of Rome. Catholicism had sealed the unanimous conscience with a new cement. This is what Claudel meant when he wrote about Rubens, the Flemish Catholic of the Counter Reformation whose work is of such a large generic nature: "It is with his whole work that we pray God, for the Protestant prays alone, but the Catholic prays in the *Church's community*." And it is a fact that already, during the same century, but in Protestant Netherlands, Rembrandt challenged this humanistic and collective nature and offered a vision of the sacred writings born from his most personal dreams. He incarnates the old Huguenot saying: "The Bible in his hand, a Protestant is a pope..." as opposed to the communion of the Catholic church (Eglise in French, as derived from "ecclesia": assembly). Confronting a religion which integrated each of its followers in general prayer and whose cult by its involved pomp aimed to exalt the conscience of a common soul, Protestantism sets up man, naked and alone, face to face with his

THE YELLOW HOUSE, 1888
Watercolor, 10″ × 12″ (25.7 × 31.7 cm)
Rijksmuseum Vincent van Gogh, Amsterdam

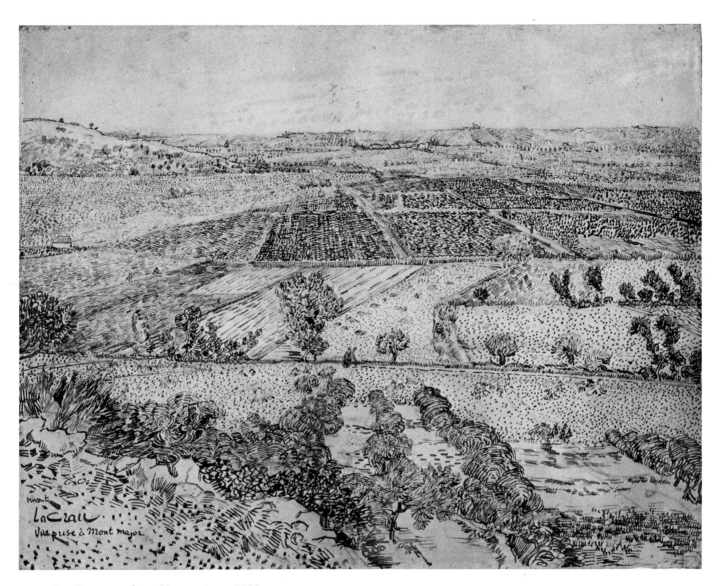

La Crau seen from Montmajour, 1888
Reed pen and black pencil, 19¼″ × 24″ (49 × 61 cm)
Rijksmuseum Vincent van Gogh, Amsterdam

The Harvest (after the *Blue Cart*), *1889*
Reed pen and ink, 9⅜″ × 12½″ (24 × 32 cm)
Collection: Mr. and Mrs. Paul Mellon
Upperville, Virginia

personal responsibilities.   The Catholic prays, or rather prayed in Latin, but the Protestant seeks a direct and controlled contact with the Scriptures in his own language.   He then finds himself alone with his own conscience.   Thus was hastened the passage from a humanistic to an individualistic culture which attained its most acute form with the 19th century.

Does anybody ever stop to think that the idea of originality, which for us has become the basis of any creative value in art or literature, was almost unintelligible during past centuries?   But at the same time that the 19th century man acquires this new conscience of originality, he has to pay for it by accepting the conscience

VAN GOGH'S BEDROOM, 1889
Oil on canvas, 22″ × 29⅛″ (56 × 74 cm)
Musée d'Orsay, Paris

Sketch of Van Gogh's Bedroom, 1888
Rijksmuseum Vincent van Gogh
Amsterdam

of loneliness and its heaviness. Starting with Chateaubriand and Romanticism, man wants to conquer his independence, refusing to owe anything to anyone but himself, and he is without protection, facing the universe alone. All that is left is I and the Other. This is when the tragedy arose — which had been brewing since the 17th century, since Blaise Pascal had first wavered between an original, strong and absorbing individualism and the Christian and Catholic collectivity in which he found a prop and an exorcism against bewilderment.

Sketch of Still Life with Coffee Pot, 1888
Rijksmuseum Vincent van Gogh
Amsterdam

Van Gogh belongs to this end of the 19th century, when the crisis arrives at its culminating point. Creative individualism becomes aggressive and anti-social. With Arthur Rimbaud's generation it becomes revolt and rebellion. But if the "Drunken Ship" can sail fervently toward unknown navigation, and if Van Gogh is in many ways close to Rimbaud's flamboyance, we must not forget that Van Gogh is a Protestant. He is torn by the same inner conflict which André Gide will know later on, with, however, quite different consequences. But this retiring into oneself goes along with a feeling of guilt. A Protestant may develop individual feelings, but he is morally aware, at the same time, of scruples. He has favored the "ego" but he has understood its dangers; his stern conscience is worried about the expansion of this ego which has no other control left than himself and which therefore must be all the more on the look-out, all the more unrelenting toward itself. This germ of discord which in another person would resolve itself into scruples, becomes for Van Gogh a heartbreak: He knows simultaneously the maximum of the ego's exaltation and the maximum of the ego's scruples. This is the source of what would be called today his failure complex. Giving himself frantically to the most intimate and most valuable part of his individuality, he is bewildered by his responsibility.

When a person becomes so centered upon himself, his balance requires that he catch up with the others and with God through an action which springs from within him and which is love: "God is love...", the Protestants incessantly state.

Ploughman in the Fields near Arles
1888-1889
Reed pen and ink
10″ × 13½″ (25.2 × 34.5 cm)
Collection: Mr. and Mrs. Paul Mellon
Upperville, Virginia

Two Houses in Saintes-Maries, 1888
Pencil and reed pen
11⅜″ × 18½″ (29 × 46 cm)
Collection
Mr. and Mrs. Eugene V. Thaw
New York

Alexandre Vinet, a Swiss theologian and one of the most eminent Protestant thinkers of the first part of the 19th century, worded thus this doubt: "Man master of himself so as to be a better servant of all?" This is really the problem of conscience which Van Gogh, after Rembrandt, transposes into artistic creation. He vehemently wants to be himself in a brutal and uncompromising way, even if he clashes with social constraint, but he sets one condition for himself: To be a better servant of all. His excessive ego is burned by a craving to *give*. His whole life is built upon an exaltation of his ego, which brings about anguish, then remorse, and finally the redemption of the ego through an act of love.

However, Van Gogh is not yet sure of the best way to shape this act of love. After the failure as an evangelist in 1872, he passes through one of the darkest periods of his life. He begins to grasp the idea of a solution through art; he makes his first friends among painters: Anton Van Rappard, whom he meets in Brussels in 1880, Anton Mauve, his cousin who agrees to guide his first steps in the Hague in 1881. But Van Gogh, discouraged by religion, tries to come back to the love of one being. During his stay with his parents in 1881 in Etten, he asked for

Public Garden Opposite the Yellow House, 1888
Reed pen, 10" × 13⅜" (25.5 × 34.5 cm)
Rijksmuseum Vincent van Gogh
Amsterdam

Farmhouse in Provence, 1888
Pencil and reed pen, 15⅜" × 21⅛" (39 × 53.7 cm)
Rijksmuseum, Rijksprintenkabinet
Amsterdam

The Sower, 1888
Pencil and reed pen, 9⅝″ × 12½″ (24.3 × 31.9 cm)
Rijksmuseum Vincent van Gogh
Amsterdam

Sketch of The Sower, 1888
Rijksmuseum Vincent van Gogh
Amsterdam

his cousin's hand and his sad rejection separates him from his family. At the time, at the beginning of 1882 in The Hague, he asks for nothing more and attempts to go to the ultimate of what he considers giving of himself. He chooses the most miserable woman he can find, the most loveless and probably the most worthless, a street girl, a drunkard, ugly, mother of five children, a woman called Christine. Undoubtedly influenced by the memories of the novels of Dostoievsky and Tolstoy he picks her up in the gutter, and, disregarding both the laws of men and morals, he takes care of her and lives with her for twenty months. This is another failure. But before leaving Christine, he takes her as the pitiful model for a lithograph made in 1882 and which he calls *Sorrow...* A naked woman, sitting with flabby breasts, heavy stomach, thin and stiff hair, and weeping with her head on her knees (see page 13).

More and more Van Gogh is under the impression that art could be the eagerly desired solution. It is precisely the richest and most complete expression of the ego but sought through work, and often through suffering, so as to enrich others by its presence. Through painting Van Gogh can become an egoist, but in the purest sense of the world, the sense Maurice Barrès gave

*Sketch of the Memory
of the Garden at Etten, 1888
Rijksmuseum Vincent van Gogh
Amsterdam*

MEMORY OF THE GARDEN
AT ETTEN, 1888
Oil on canvas
29″ × 36⅜″ (73.5 × 92.5 cm)
The Hermitage Museum
Leningrad

*Thistles Along
the Roadside, 1888
Reed pen and pencil
9⅝″ × 12⅝″
(24.3 × 32 cm)
Rijksmuseum
Vincent van Gogh
Amsterdam*

to egotism.   He will give himself to his ego, he will let himself be possesed by it, but only to draw out all the riches it contains.   He cuts out from his bleeding personality the pound of flesh which he intends throwing out to feed the others. The equation is resolved: Exaltation equals giving.   But as nothing must be easy for him, he will have to plow deeply and for a long time this barren field before the first green sprout, the one which will bear flowers, bursts from this torn soil.

Van Gogh belongs to the family of seers, greatest poets, greatest painters.   For them the false antagonism which our times has planted between the abstract and figurative art does not exist.   The seer no longer registers reality as a mere show, by looking mechanically, as most men do.   Beyond the sensory aspect of things which satisfies the positive vision, he can perceive what they mean, what they are.   This gift, which was mere instinct before, has become conscious and has been cultivated since Charles Baudelaire.   The Symbolists, and Van Gogh is one, made it the basis of art.   Any real artist *chooses*, without even knowing it, among all the things which life shows and brings, only what a secret correlation connects with his own nature.   Objects are no longer solely a story, a thing passing in front of his eyes by chance; he watches out, he listens to a harmony, to a vibration, wherein he recognizes himself, where often even he becomes clearer, and which, underlined, freed, brings to others the echo of what vibrates in his sensibility.

With Paul Gauguin who announced "the musical part which color will now have in modern painting," Van Gogh will soon be predicting: "Painting, such as it is now, promises to become more subtle — more music and less sculpture — and especially it promises color." It is color — "a vibration as is music" writes Gauguin in 1899 — which he will mostly use during his last years to express his perception of the world. He explains in 1888 to his brother Theo that he wanted to "express the love of two lovers by a marriage between two complementary colors, their mixture, their oppositions, the mysterious vibrations of close tints. Express the thought of a forehead by the spreading out of a light tone on a dark background." He adds: "I tried to express with red and green the terrible human passions." But before discovering painting which "Like sorcerers and magnetizers, project its thoughts at a distance" — as Baudelaire said when speaking of Delacroix paintings — he already tries to clear out the deeper meaning of things through the choice of objects and the subject.

Rocks with Trees:
Montmajour, 1888
Reed pen
India ink and pencil
19¼" × 23⅝"
(49 × 60 cm)
Rijksmuseum
Vincent van Gogh
Amsterdam

In his first paintings, especially from 1882 on, and which will be his Dutch period, he is faithful to the life of the poor. But he is no longer satisfied, as in his earlier drawings, to trace some striking but anecdotical episodes as, for instance, this long black line of miners going to work through the snow. He is obsessed by the symbolical strength of these endlessly repeated themes: "The man from the bottom of the abyss, *De Profundis*, is the coal-miner, the other one with a dreamy, almost thoughtful, almost sleep-walking expression is the weaver." The first one "Tears out from the bowels of the earth this mineral substance whose great necessity we all know." The weaver, surrounded by a web of poles and threads, materializes these "prisoners in I know not what horrible cage," which we saw him mention before (see page 11). The simplest, most miserable, most scorned object takes on a violent bearing. Quite often Van Gogh will paint some shoes, old worn out shoes. Broken down, out of shape, gaping and deeply furrowed by wear they express the misery of walking bodies and of toil; they are weariness itself. In the same way he does not paint — not yet — flowers, but potatoes, loamy, buried in the soil from which they will have to be torn away, just as coal, to palliate men's destitution. He finds himself akin to those shapeless tubers in their hard fight to bloom! As far back as in 1878 he felt rising in him the expressive strength of beings and things fighting in the dark to shoot up toward brightness. "You know, he wrote to his brother, that one of the roots of not only, the Gospel's but of the whole Bible's fundamental truth is: 'From darkness to light'." *Per tenebras ad lucem!* This is already the meaning of all of his life, of his long journey into night; it is the re-discovery of the truth stated by the great mystics: Only by deserving it in going through darkness can one reach the great lights... He knows this already: "Experience proves that those working in the dark, in the middle of the earth, as the miners in the black pits, are easily moved by the word of the Gospel and believe it with no effort."

His first great painting, in 1885, sums up all this: *The Potato Eaters* are

Olive Trees at Montmajour, 1888
Pencil and reed pen, 18⅞" × 23½" (48 × 60 cm)
Musée des Beaux-Arts, Tournai, Belgium

peasants, brothers of the miners. Worn out at the end of a day of toil, greedy and uncouth, sitting around the table, they hanker after the steaming dish of humble food. (see page 9).

From then on, Van Gogh too is leading toward light, color, the sun. In 1885 his father died, and so did his past life. Vincent starts his progressive march toward the South. In November he arrives in Antwerp, Flemish land, land of the Counter-Reformation, Rubens, exuberant joy of living. Moreover, he discovers there the first Japanese etchings which are coming to Europe and are bringing about a change in taste. The time is close when he will abandon the "brown tones, for instance of bitumen and bistre" which alone could express the sad underground smoldering of his art.

In March 1886 he is in Paris and is hit by Impressionism. He works in Cormont's studio where he meets Henri de Toulouse-Lautrec and soon makes friend with Gauguin, Camille Pissarro and Georges Seurat. The latest Impressionist exhibition is just taking place at Durand-Ruel's gallery. However, it is through Adolphe Monticelli, — whose heavy and powerful technique, clay impastement, chromatic and almost mineral resonance, he imitates — that he

Meadow with Flowers, 1888
Pencil and reed pen
10″ × 13⅝″ (25.5 × 34.5 cm)
Rijksmuseum Vincent van Gogh
Amsterdam

Path through a Field with Willows, 1888
Pencil and pen
10″ × 13⅝″ (25.5 × 34.5 cm)
Rijksmuseum Vincent van Gogh
Amsterdam

49

THE NIGHT CAFÉ, 1888
Oil on canvas
28½″ × 36¼″ (72.5 × 92 cm)
The Yale University Art Gallery
New Haven, Connecticut
Bequest of Stephen C. Clark

Tree with Ivy in the Asylum Garden, 1889. Pencil, chalk and reed pen, 24″ × 18¼″ (62 × 47 cm)
Rijksmuseum Vincent van Gogh, Amsterdam

LES ALYSCAMPS, 1888.   Oil on canvas, 36⅝″ × 28⅜″ (93 × 72 cm)
Private collection

Wheat Field with Sun and Cloud, 1889
Black chalk and reed pen heightened with white chalk, 18¼″ × 22″ (47.5 × 56 cm)
Rijksmuseum Kröller-Müller, Otterlo

discovers both flowers and color.   But the Impressionists lead him toward light which he can see emerging in its Parisian subtility.   The shoot has broken through the earth's hard crust: It is now irresistibly drawn toward the sun.

Where can he find it?   Through the Japanese engravings he gets glimpses of the Orient, the Empie of the Rising Sun.   "So how could one not go to Japan, that is to its equivalent, the South?" On February 21, 1888, he is in Arles; he finds snow there, but a light and luminous snow which prepares him for the precocious

Sketch of Garden with Weeping Willow
Rijksmuseum Vincent van Gogh
Amsterdam

he was groping through his primary darkness, but on a land to which he was not native, and where it was not natural for him to live. Like Greco, he will be torn between his hereditary and physical being, and the imaginary being he carries within, and to which life was offering an unexpected chance of materializing itself. Neither his system nor his sensibility are built for such heady circumstances — despite the fact he craves for them — so he gets drunk to the point of madness

Public Garden with Fence, 1888
Pencil, reed pen and India ink
12⅝" × 9⅝" (32 × 24.3 cm)
Rijksmuseum Vincent van Gogh
Amsterdam

spring of the Provence, its flowers, the white dust of its orchards, "Something gay and tender." For the first time, perhaps, Van Gogh is happy; he paints the white, innumerable petals, the apple trees puffed up with a white and pink brightness; he paints this swarming of sparkling coolness. The die is cast. He will be a prey for the sun he sought for, unprotected against it, almost uprooted; more so than Greco, and like him frantic, on the brink of insanity, dizziness. He is seeing his passionate, glaring dream come true, this dream toward which

PORTRAIT OF CAMILLE ROULIN, 1888
Oil on canvas, 14¾″ × 12¾″ (37.5 × 32.5 cm)
Rijksmuseum Vincent van Gogh, Amsterdam

Sketch of Stagecoach of Tarascon, 1888
Rijksmuseum Vincent van Gogh
Amsterdam

PORTRAIT OF A MAN, 1888.   Oil on canvas, 25¼″ × 21½″ (65 × 54.6 cm)
Rijksmuseum Kröller-Müller, Otterlo

L'ARLÉSIENNE: MADAME GINOUX, 1888.   Oil on canvas, 36″ × 29″ (93 × 74 cm)
The Metropolitan Museum of Art, New York. Bequest of Sam A. Lewisohn

and death. Paul Cézanne's story is exactly the opposite. When he arrived in this same Provence — from where he originated — all he had to do was to scratch the soil a little in order to get closer to his own roots and to discover himself. Under the scorching intensity of this sun he will achieve harmony, whereas Van Gogh will burn himself out.

Van Gogh now becomes the prey of the sun and during the three years left to him, he will in a curious way follow its seasonal rhythm. He bursts out with spring, reaches his highest point during summer and discovers July and the

PORTRAIT OF ARMAND ROULIN, 1888.   Oil on canvas, 26″ × 21⅝″ (66 × 55 cm)
Museum Folkwang, Essen

flame's plenitude. The sign of the fire will show in his color brought by a breathless and melting touch of red and blue to yellow, "A sun, a light, that for lack of a better name I can only call yellow, pale sulphur yellow, pale lemon. How beautiful is yellow!" With a kind of obsession he multiplies, to decorate his studio, large paintings of sunflowers, so called because of their shape, color, heliotropism. In them he recognizes himself. And in his landscapes he often draws, behind haystacks — another deeply significant symbol — the fiery globe in the sky, as Claude Le Lorrain used to do. At this time of plenitude and happiness, it seems he has exorcised the malediction of the man alone. Impressionism had already suggested to him the idea of group painting, where the gifts of each and every one would plunge back into community. He wants paintings "to go beyond the power of one man." This is when he dreams of founding in Arles this "Studio of the South" where, with Gauguin who will answer his call, Charles Laval and Emile Bernard were also supposed to join him.

He also goes beyond himself because he discovers universal life. "I am painting infinity." From the rock of Montmajour, he no longer sees a foggy northern plain, with lost visibility, preliminary shape of something unlimited, but a large shadowless space, entirely visible in its smallest details. This represents at the same time the infinitely vast, the plain stretching beyond what the eye can see, and the infinitely small, the multiplication of fields, olive groves, vineyards, stones, where life swarms with a dust of visible marks, myriads of microscopic pores of the earth's face, (see drawings pages 38 and 39).

It is now the zenith of July: "I feel inside me a strength which I must

Chair Near the Stove, 1888
Pencil, 13″ × 10″ (32 × 25 cm)
Rijksmuseum Vincent van Gogh
Amsterdam

Gauguin's Chair, 1888. Oil on canvas, 37⅞″ × 28⅛″ (90.5 × 72 cm)
Rijksmuseum Vincent van Gogh, Amsterdam

SELF-PORTRAIT WITH BANDAGED EAR AND PIPE, 1889
Oil on canvas, 20⅛″ × 17¾″ (51 × 45 cm).   Private collection

expand, a fire which I cannot put out, but which I must nurture, although I don't know to which exit it will lead, and I would not be astonished if it were a dark one". He feels he is dedicated to the fire, but he knows at the same time that the end of any fire is ashes. His color, which one might believe freed from their original shadows, develops. The cypress, this dark and funeral tree, starts appearing. Soon the pure yellows, the yellows of Vermeer which he used at the beginning, glide toward the reddish-brown of haystacks. Then they change into copper, and from copper into bronze.

The tragedy starts. The new Icarus can soar toward the sun, but he will weaken and fall. He can cry, as in Baudelaire's verses:

> Under I do not know what fiery eye
> I feel my wing breaking.

Gauguin arrives in Arles on October 28, 1888. Enthusiasm is soon replaced by quarrels. Van Gogh finds out that the ego remains incompatible, and even incommunicable. Moneyless, he does not eat every day. Only spirits can sustain him, and excited by absinth taken on an empty stomach, he stays for hours working under a glaring sun, not made for his northern head. Here comes the winter

Carriage Drawn by a Horse, 1889-1890. Black chalk, 8½″ × 10″ (20.5 × 24 cm)
Rijksmuseum Vincent van Gogh, Amsterdam

STILL LIFE WITH ONIONS, 1889
Oil on canvas, 19¾″ × 25¼″ (50 × 64 cm)
Rijksmuseum Kröller-Müller, Otterlo

Still Life with Oranges, Lemons and Blue Gloves, 1889
Oil on canvas, 18⅞″ × 24¾″ (48 × 62 cm)
Collection: Mr. and Mrs. Paul Mellon, Upperville, Virginia

*Corridor of Saint-Paul Asylum in
Saint-Rémy, 1889
Black chalk and gouache
26" × 19½" (61.5 × 47 cm)
The Museum of Modern Art, New York*

PRISONERS' ROUND
(after an engraving by GUSTAVE DORÉ), 1890
Oil on canvas, 32" × 25½" (80 × 64 cm)
Pushkin State Museum of Fine Arts
Moscow

*La Roubine du Roi with
Washerwomen, 1888
Reed pen, 12½" × 10" (31 × 24 cm)
Rijksmuseum Vincent van Gogh
Amsterdam*

solestice! Three days later, on December 24, Van Gogh throws his glass into Gauguin's face. The next day, as Gauguin is walking in the street, he hears rapid footsteps behind him, turns around and beholds Van Gogh, holding a razor and marching on him. Gauguin stares him to a halt; then, Van Gogh runs away. He runs home and, back in his room, he cuts off his ear with the razor, wraps it up in a handkerchief, and goes out to offer it to a brothel's wench. The

The Reaper (after MILLET), 1889.   Oil on canvas, 17⅛″ × 13¼″ (43.5 × 33.5 cm)
Rijksmuseum Vincent van Gogh, Amsterdam

PEASANT WOMAN BINDING THE WHEAT IN SHEAVES (AFTER MILLET), 1889
Oil on canvas, 17½″ × 13½″ (43.5 × 33.5 cm).   Stedelijk Museum, Amsterdam

THE SCHOOLBOY, 1890.   Oil on canvas, 25″ × 21¼″ (63.5 × 54 cm)
Museu de Arte, São Paulo, Brazil

Man Digging and other
Figure Studies, 1889
Pencil and black chalk
9″ × 12¼″ (22.9 × 31.1 cm)
Collection
Mr. and Mrs. Eugene V. Thaw
New York

Saint-Rémy, Workers in the Field, 1889
Pencil and black chalk
9″ × 12¼″ (22.9 × 31.1 cm)
Collection
Mr. and Mrs. Eugene V. Thaw
New York

Walking, 1889-1890.   Pencil, 10″ × 13″ (24.5 × 32 cm)
Rijksmuseum Vincent van Gogh, Amsterdam

motivation of this act has been discussed at length.   Transposed on Vincent's then extraordinary nervous over-excitment, it appears perfectly coherent with everything we know about him.   He failed once more in his dream of a collective studio, and in his dream of friendship.   Failure and guilt...   His action calls to the mind, Lafcadio's self-punishing penknife stabs, imagined by André Gide, another Protestant...   Punishment is linked with the idea of self-gift and of the gift of sacrifice to the humble: This is why he will go and take to the lowest woman, to this sister of Christine, this piece of flesh which he cut from himself as a punishment.   The year 1889 starts with his internment first in Arles, then in the St. Rémy Asylum, on May 9.   Spring has started the solar cycle again.   Now that the balance is broken, the frenzy which already rose in Arles is amplified: "The row of bushes at the end are all rose-laurel, raving mad; the damp plants

Corner of the Park, 1889-1890
Pencil, 8" × 12" (20 × 29.5 cm)
Rijksmuseum Vincent van Gogh
Amsterdam

The Cabriolet, 1889
Black chalk, 13½" × 11" (28 × 24 cm)
Rijksmuseum Vincent van Gogh
Amsterdam

Rocks with Oak Tree, 1889
Pen reed, 8⅜" × 12¼" (24 × 31 cm)
Private collection

are blossoming in such a way, that they should indeed catch a locomotor ataxy... Their greenery too, renews itself by vigorous new shoots, which seem inexhaustible..."

The solar blaze changes him into a real burning bush. His mind gives itself away to a dizziness which is beginning to intoxicate him. Panorama's infinitiy takes on a hallucinatory nature. Life which he sensed everywhere, starts shaking, starts moving. It upsets shapes, it ripples, it swells like an ocean under the ground's shell. It intensifies everything. The enormous multiplication of grass, of leaves, space rushing, dashing toward the horizon like a fireball, the movements of the earth which crawls, wells, rocks, the movements

Peasants at the Table, 1889-1890
Pencil, 10″ × 13″ (24.5 × 32 cm)
Rijksmuseum Vincent van Gogh
Amsterdam

Interior, 1889
Black chalk, 11″ × 12″ (25 × 24.5 cm)
Private collection

76

of the leaves overlapping each other, breaking loose with the suction of air. In a sort of general vibration, everything rocks and tumbles, everything spreads in a breathtaking dizziness which is the breath of the universe itself freed from all contraint. But ashes are already dimming the fire. Everywhere now, cypresses, which still leap up like sparks toward the sky, bring with them the color of the night. Before the end of the summer, violet and pale blue colors are here, there and everywhere about the olive trees. Behind the dying flowers the crackling of the dying fire can be heard. He shudders: "Careful of the feast's tomorrows, careful of the winter mistral!..."[1] The results of this terrible attack are that my mind hardly harbors any more clear desire or hope. I wonder whether this is how one feels, with passions dimmed out, one comes down from the mountain

(1) A cold wind that blows in the South of France.

In Front of the Fireplace, 1889-1890. Black chalk, 9″ × 13″ (23.5 × 32 cm)
Rijksmuseum Vincent van Gogh, Amsterdam

OLIVE TREES WITH THE ALPILLES
IN THE BACKGROUND, 1889
Oil on canvas, 28½″ × 36¼″ (72.5 × 92 cm)
Collection: Mrs. John Hay Whitney, New York

LANDSCAPE WITH COUPLE WALKING AND CRESCENT MOON, 1889
Oil on canvas, 19½″ × 17⅞″ (49.5 × 45.5 cm)
Museu de Arte, São Paulo, Brazil

PORTRAIT OF DR. GACHET, 1890
Oil on canvas, 26¾″ × 22½″ (68 × 57 cm)
Musée d'Orsay, Paris

Mademoiselle Gachet at the Piano, 1890
Black pencil, 12½″ × 9½″ (30 × 19 cm)
Rijksmuseum Vincent van Gogh
Amsterdam

instead of climbing up?" He comes back to a subject he had painted in 1882: "Getting ready for the great journey," a desperate old man, holding his head. Sun is out of the question. The old man is sitting near a poor fireplace where a smoky spit is still burning, but about to go out.

Then stalked by illness, haunted by the desperation to win, he flees toward the north, toward his native sky. So strong is the pining for his youth that he even speaks of coming back to the gray coloring of his debut. He runs to hide the mortal wound made to him by the sun. Near Paris, by Pontoise, in Auvers, he puts himself into Dr. Gachet's hands. The doctor was recommended by his brother. This is May 1890. The frantic violence of his paintbrush spurts and spreads out as never before, but like waves breaking on a rock. Look at it closely: The dazzling arabesques of older days are replaced by a restive graphism, by small, stiff, broken, almost forced sticks. The brushstroke, as the outline, is somewhat broken and breathless. One can feel, that physically, muscularly, nervously, the

Study of a Fruit Tree, 1890
Black chalk, 12½″ × 9½″ (31 × 24 cm)
Rijksmuseum Vincent van Gogh
Amsterdam

Study Sheets, 1890
Black pencil and lilac colored ink
9″ × 12″ (23.5 × 30 cm)
Rijksmuseum Vincent van Gogh
Amsterdam

hand no longer responds. The painting may thus acquire something more powerful, tragic and moving. Van Gogh can guess it is the end; he is on his way down from the mountain. "Here, having come back, I started working again, the brush almost falling out of my hand — and knowing exactly what I wanted, I still painted three large canvases." He still wants, he still conceives, with perhaps more genius than ever, but the hand slips away. And what are those canvases? "Vast fields of wheat under troubled skies. I had no scruples trying to express sadness, extreme loneliness" (see page 90).

Crows Over the Wheat Field! In Paris, when he was rising toward the sun, he would throw a merry skylark on golden wheat. Now the wheat is almost brown, made of touches which, in their utmost vehemence, seem to coagulate and to break themselves. Now he can only see the ravens. And because this time the crescendo of summer did not lead him anywhere, on July 27, 1890, he shoots himself in the chest. With his silent courage, he comes back, leaving behind a bloody trail in the dust, goes up to his room, in the café where he lived, lays down like a wounded animal, and like a wolf in his den, he calmly starts dying.

Sketch of Thatched Cottages at Auvers, 1890
Rijksmuseum Vincent van Gogh, Amsterdam

Peasant Woman in a Wheat Field, 1890
Black pencil, 12" × 9" (30.5 × 23.5 cm)
Rijksmuseum Vincent van Gogh, Amsterdam

Dr. Gachet rushes to his side, stays up with him, hopes to save him, but two days later, complications set in and Vincent dies. He had scribbled these last words for his brother Theo: "For my own work I am risking my life, and my mind is half gone... But what do you want?"

But what do you want?

THE CHURCH AT AUVERS, 1890
Oil on canvas, 37″ × 29⅛″ (94 × 74 cm)
Musée d'Orsay, Paris

A Hut, 1890
Blue pencil, 9½″ × 12½″ (24 × 31 cm)
Rijksmuseum Vincent van Gogh
Amsterdam

The question is open on a white sheet of paper where no answer was ever to be written, except the answer of fame.

Thus was the life of Van Gogh. Absolute failure for him, sublime success for us, but he never knew it: "Under some circumstances it is better to be the loser than the winner, it is better to be Prometheus than Jupiter." Vanquished, maybe! But through a defeat which is the most beautiful of victories. Yes, complete failure: In individual love, in collective love, in pictural endeavour (could he think otherwise? He, who almost never sold any of his pictures, who saw those he offered either rejected or neglected!) physical and moral failure of a system and a mind both ruined at the age where others reach their plenitude.

Is it not the picture of a completely wasted life? He must have felt it such to go to the end of what was his destiny: That is a total gift of himself, the redemption of his ego, exalted by the total sacrifice of everything which he had a right to expect. Van Gogh will have lived this admirable and perhaps unique passion;

A House at Auvers, 1890
Pencil, 17⅜″ × 10⅝″ (44.5 × 27.5 cm)
Rijksmuseum Vincent van Gogh, Amsterdam

The Town Hall at Auvers, 1890
Black pencil
9⅜″ × 12⅛″ (24 × 31 cm)
Rijksmuseum Vincent van Gogh
Amsterdam

he will have greedily educated and developed his ego and will not have gotten anything out of it for himself but disappointment and finally the excruciating feeling of having achieved nothing in this life — a useless life. But is is because of this that he is so great, because of this that his genius appears to us with the purity of a saint of painting. For, when he assumed his own nothingness, he started becoming for others, for ever increasing multitudes, a warming and illuminating fire. This lost fire, hardly noticeable by a barren smoke, has now changed into a sun, a sun whirling in our eyes and in our hearts and projecting its splendor — splendor made of flame, of love, of life.

WHEAT FIELD UNDER A CLOUDED SKY, 1890
Oil on canvas
19⅝″ × 39½″ (50 × 100 cm)
Rijksmuseum Vincent van Gogh
Amsterdam

BIOGRAPHY

1853   Vincent Willem van Gogh was born on March 30 in Zundert, in the Brabant. He was the son of a Protestant minister and grew up in a religious atmosphere. Three of his uncles were art dealers.

1869   Began to work for the Goupil Gallery in its various branches in The Hague, London, and Paris.

1876-1877   Emotional instability led to his dismissal in the spring of 1876. He decided to devote his life to the poor. He left for England, where he held minor jobs in schools and worked as an assistant to a clergyman. He began to study theology in Amsterdam but he found himself unable to take the examinations for admission to the university. He then settled in the Belgian mining district of the Borinage, where, as a lay minister, he shared the miners' wretched existence.

1879   Period of aimless wandering.

1880-1881   Studied drawing in Brussels and copied several works by Millet. He was also influenced by Dutch artists, among whom his cousin Anton Mauve. First drawings with a reed pen. Started using oil paints at the end of the year. Stay with his parents in Etten.

1881-1882   Stay at The Hague. His uncle, the art dealer C.M. van Gogh, commissioned him for views of the city. He chose to depict a factory, a bakery and a gasworks.

1883   Stay in Drenthe.

1883-1885   Lived with his parents in Nuenen, in Northern Brabant. He roamed the countryside, sketching and painting the peasants and their surroundings. *The Potato Eaters.*

1885   Death of his father on March 26. Van Gogh settled in Antwerp in November. He studied at the Academy and discovered the works of Rubens. He was also influenced by the colors and composition of Japanese prints.

1886   Arrived in Paris in March. He settled with his brother Theo, who was working with the firm Boussod & Valadon.

1886-1888   Met Toulouse-Lautrec and Emile Bernard at Cormon's studio. Became friends with Gauguin, Pissarro, and Seurat. Exchanged paintings with Gauguin. During this period, he produced over two hundred paintings. His colors became lighter under the influence of the Impressionists. Collected Japanese prints. *Portrait of Père Tanguy.* Landscapes of Montmartre.

1887   Spring and summer: series of landscapes with the bridge at Asnières, the Restaurant de la Grève, and the factories at Asnières. Organized a show of Japanese prints at the Café Tambourin, on the Boulevard Clichy. In the fall, started to copy Japanese prints.

1888   Visited Seurat's studio with Theo. He settled in Arles on February 20, and he lived there until May 8, 1889. During this period, he painted two hundred oils and produced over a hundred drawings and watercolors. Boarded at the Hôtel-Restaurant Carrel.

March   Series of *Orchards in Bloom.* Three paintings were shown at the Salon des Indépendants.

April   Drawings with reed pen.

May   Rented the Yellow House, at 2 Place Lamartine. He still lived in a hotel, the Café de la Gare, where he remained until September. *View of Arles with Irises in the Foreground* and the *Langlois Bridge.* Drawings of the Abbaye de Montmajour.

June   Stay at Saintes-Maries. Started a series of paintings on the theme of the harvest: ten paintings made between June 13 and 24. *The Harvest (The Blue Cart), The Sower, Haystacks, The Roubine du Roi with Washerwomen, The Zouave.* Suggested that Gauguin join him at Arles and hoped to found an artists' colony.

July   Stay at Montmajour: second series of drawings. *The Mousmé.* Met the postman, Joseph Roulin. Made thirty-two drawings after his oils.

August   *Portrait of Roulin, Quay with Men Unloading Sand Barges.*

September   *The Night Café.* Made arrangements for Gauguin's arrival: he bought furniture, had gaslight installed, and found a cleaning woman. He moved into the Yellow House.

October   Painted fifteen oils from mid-August on. The series of *Sunflowers* and *The Poet's Garden.* Gauguin arrived on October 23. *Les Alyscamps.*

November   *The Vineyard.* At first, the two artists worked on the same motif and shared the same model. Mid-November, Gauguin encouraged Van Gogh to paint from memory. Several paintings showing both the tutelage of and a rivalry with Gauguin. Portraits of the other members of the Roulin family.

December   Gauguin and Van Gogh have more and more bitter quarrels, which threaten Van Gogh's fragile balance. Gauguin resolved to return to Paris. After a violent dispute with Gauguin on the 24th, Van Gogh slashed one of his own ears. He was admitted at the Hôtel Dieu. Gauguin left for Paris.

January   Left the hospital on the 7th and immediately resumed painting. *La Berceuse.*

February   He suffered from hallucinations and was in constant fear of being poisoned. He was taken to the hospital and placed in an isolated room. He remained ten days there and returned home. His neighbors signed a petition that he be admitted to a mental asylum.

March   Taken to the hospital. Signac visited him.

April   Decided to go to the hospital at Saint-Rémy.

May   Began drawing again with a reed pen. On May 8, he left for the asylum of Saint-Paul-de Mausole at Saint-Rémy. He was to stay there until May 20, 1890. In spite of several bouts of illness, he painted one-hundred-and-fifty oils and made several hundred drawings. Series of *The Garden of the Asylum.* Many landscapes in a very lyrical style. Theme of the cypress tree.

October   Paintings after Millet.

November   Series of *Olive Orchards.*

January   Several paintings by Van Gogh were shown at the Salon des XX in Brussels.

March   Ten oils at the Salon des Indépendants. Ill again. Made small drawings.

April   Continued to paint in spite of his illness: landscapes of the Brabant.

May 1890   Left for Paris on May 16, where he stayed with his brother. He arrived at Auvers-sur-Oise on the 20th, with a letter of recommendation for Dr. Gachet. At Auvers he was to paint over seventy oils.

June   *The Church at Auvers, Peasant Woman with a Straw Hat Sitting in the Wheat.*

July   *Crows over the Wheat Field, Daubigny's Garden.* Van Gogh shot himself on July 27 and died two days later.

BIBLIOGRAPHY

LETTERS

The *Letters to His Brother Theo* (652) were published by Johanna van Gogh-Bonger en three volumes: *Brieven aan zijn broeder.* Amsterdam, 1914-1925. In English, translated in part by Johanna van Gogh-Bonger: *Letters of Vincent van Gogh to His Brother, 1872-1889.* London, Boston, New York: Houghton Mifflin, 1927-1929. Several letters are in French.

Letters to Anton Ridder van Rappart, 1881-1885 (58). Trans. by Rela van Messel. New York: Viking, 1936.

Letters to Emile Bernard (21). Ed., trans., and with a foreword by Douglas Lord. London, New York: Museum of Modern Art, 1938.

Briefe an Emile Bernard, Paul Gauguin, Paul Signac und andere. Ed. by Hans Graber. Basel: Schwabe, 1938.

Vincent van Gogh raconté par lui même et par ses amis, ses contemporains, sa postérité. Ed. by Pierre Courthion. Vézenaz, Geneva: Cailler, 1947.

Verzamelde Brieven van Vincent van Gogh. Amsterdam: Wereld-Bibliothek, 1952-1955. In English: *The Complete Letters of Vincent van Gogh.* With reproduction of all the drawings featured in the correspondence. Amsterdam: Wereld-Bibliothek, 1952-1955. Greenwich, Connecticut: New York Graphic Society, 1958.

Lettres de Vincent van Gogh à sa mère (8). French trans. by Louis Roëlandt. Paris: Falaize, 1952.

Als Mensch unter Menschen: Vincent van Gogh in seinen Briefen an den Bruder Theo. Letters by Fritz Erpel. East-Berlin: Henschelverlag, 1959.

Vincent van Gogh, a Self-Portrait. Ed. by W.H. Auden. Greenwich, Connecticut: New York Graphic Society, 1961.

The Letters of Vincent van Gogh. Ed. by Mark W. Roskill. New York: Atheneum, 1963.

Letters of Vincent van Gogh, 1886-1890 : A Facsimile Edition. Preface by J. Leymarie. Int. by V.W. van Gogh. London: Scholar Press, 1977.

KARAGHEUSIAN, A. *Vincent van Gogh's Letters Written in French: Differences Between the Printed Versions and the Manuscripts.* New York, 1984.

CATALOGUES RAISONNÉS

LA FAILLE, J.-B. de. *L'Œuvre de Vincent van Gogh : Catalogue raisonné.* 4 vols. Paris, Brussels: G. van Oest, 1928. Rev. ed.: *The Works of Vincent van Gogh, His Paintings and Drawings.* Amsterdam : Meulenhoff; New York : Reynal & Morrow, 1970.

SCHERJON, W. and GRUYTER, W.J. de. *Vincent van Gogh's Great Period: Arles, Saint-Rémy and Auvers-sur-Oise.* Amsterdam: De Spieghel, 1937.

LA FAILLE, J.-B. de. *Vincent van Gogh.* Paris, London, New York: Hyperion, 1939.

HULSKER, Jan. *Van Gogh en zijn weg.* Amsterdam : Meulenhoff, 1977. English ed.: *The Complete Van Gogh: Paintings, Drawings, Sketches.* New York: Abrams, 1980.

GENERAL

ALETRINO, Paul. *Vincent van Gogh.* Milan: Rizzoli, 1980.

ARTAUD, Antonin. *Van Gogh, le suicidé de la société.* Paris, 1947.

AURIER, G.A., *Œuvres posthumes.* Paris: Mercure de France, 1893.

BADER, Alfred. *Künstler-Tragik. Karl Stauffer, Vincent van Gogh.* Basel: Schwabe, 1932.

BADT, Kurt. *Die Farbenlehre Van Goghs.* Cologne: DuMont, 1961.

BEER, François J. *Les Rapports de l'art et de la maladie de Van Gogh.* Doctoral thesis, Strasbourg, 1935.

BEER, François J. *Du Démon de Van Gogh. Avec Van Gogh à l'asile* by E. LEROY. Nice: A.I.D.A.; Lyons: Cartier, 1945.

BEUCKEN, Jean de. *Un Portrait de Vincent van Gogh.* Liège: Balancier, 1938.

BIERMANN, Georg. *Vincent van Gogh, mit einem Auszug aus den Briefen an seiner Bruder Theo.* Munich: K. Desch, 1949.

BREMMER, H.P. *Vincent van Gogh inleidende beschouwingen.* Amsterdam: W. Versluys, 1911.

BUCHMANN, Mark. *Die Farbe bei Vincent van Gogh.* Zurich: Bibliander, 1948.

CABANNE, Pierre. *Van Gogh. L'Homme et son œuvre.* Paris, 1961. *Van Gogh. Trans. by Mary Martin. Englewood Cliffs, New Jersey: Prentice Hall, 1961.*

CASSOU, Jean and REWALD, John. *Vincent van Gogh.* Paris: La Renaissance, 1937.

CATESSON, J. *Considérations sur la folie de Van Gogh.* Doctoral thesis, Paris, 1943.

CHETHAM, Charles S. *The Role of Vincent van Gogh's Copies in the Development of His Art.* London, New York: Garland, 1976.

COGNIAT, Raymond. *Van Gogh.* Paris, 1953. Trans. by James Cleugh. New York: Abrams, 1959.

COLIN, Paul. *Van Gogh.* Paris: Rieder, 1925. Trans. by Beatrice Moggridge. London, 1926.

COOPER, Douglas. *Drawings and Watercolors by Vincent van Gogh.* Preceded by the essay *The Colors* by Hugo von Hofmannsthal. New York: Macmillan, 1955.

COQUIOT, Gustave. *Vincent van Gogh.* Paris: Ollendorf, 1923.

CROSS, John E. *Vincent van Gogh.* New York: Atheneum, 1947.

DESCARGUES, Pierre. *Vincent van Gogh.* Paris: Cercle d'art, 1975. New York: Abrams, 1975

DOITEAU, Victor and LEROY, Edgard. *La Folie de Vincent van Gogh.* Paris: Esculape, 1928.

DOITEAU, Victor and LEROY, Edgard. *Van Gogh et le drame de l'oreille coupée.* Paris: Esculape, 1936.

DORNER, Alexander. *Vincent van Gogh. Blumen und Landschaften.* Berlin: Klein, 1937.

DU QUESNE-VAN GOGH, E.H. *Persoonlijke Herinneringen aan Vincent van Gogh.* Baarn: J.F. van der Ven, 1910. English trans., London:Constable, 1913.

DURET, Théodore. *Vincent van Gogh.* Paris: Bernheim-Jeune, 1916, 1919.

EARP, Thomas Wade. *Van Gogh.* London, Edimburg: Nelson & Black, 1934.

ELGAR, Frank. *Van Gogh Peintures.* Paris, 1947.

ELGAR, Frank. *Van Gogh*. Paris: Hazan, 1958. *Van Gogh, A Study of His Life and Work*. Trans. by James Cleugh, New York: Praeger, 1958.

ERPEL, Fritz. *Die Sebstbildnisse Vincent van Goghs*. Berlin, 1963. *Van Gogh, the Self-Portraits*. Trans. by Doris Edwards. Greenwich, Connecticut: New York Graphic Society, 1969.

ESTIENNE, Charles and SIBERT, C.H. *Van Gogh*. Geneva: Skira, 1953. Engl. trans. by S.J.C. Harrison.

EVAN, Grose. *Van Gogh*. New York: McGraw Hill, 1968.

FELS, Florent. *Vincent van Gogh*. Paris: Stock, 1924; Floury, 1928.

FIERENS, Paul. *Vincent van Gogh*. Paris: Braun, 1947.

FLORISOONE, Michel. *Van Gogh*. Paris: Plon, 1937.

FRANK, Herbert. *Vincent van Gogh in Selbstzeugnissen und Bilddokumenten*. Reinbeck/Hamburg: Rowohlt, 1976.

GACHET, Paul. *Souvenirs de Cézanne et Vincent van Gogh*. Paris, 1953.

GACHET, PAUL. *Vincent van Gogh aux Indépendants*. Paris, 1953.

GACHET, Paul. *Deux amis des impressionnistes: le Dr. Gachet et Murer*. Paris: Musées nationaux, 1956.

GACHET, Paul. *Lettres impressionnistes au Dr. Gachet et à Murer*. Paris, 1957.

GACHET, Paul and BAZIN, Germain. *Van Gogh et les peintres d'Auvers-sur-Oise*. Catalogue d'exposition, Musée de l'Orangerie, Paris, 1954.

GERSON, Horst. *Voor en an Van Gogh*. Amsterdam: Contact, 1961.

GLASER, Curt. *Vincent van Gogh*. Leipzig: Seeman, 1921.

GOLDSCHEIDER, Ludwig and UHDE, W. *Vincent van Gogh*. Paris: Phaidon, 1936. New York: Oxford University Press, 1941.

GOLDSCHEIDER, Ludwig. *Van Gogh. Paintings and Drawings*. Oxford, London, 1947.

GRAETZ, H. *The Symbolic Language of Vincent van Gogh*. London, 1963.

GREY, Roch. *Van Gogh*. Rome: Valori Plastici; Paris: Crès, 1924.

GROHN, Hans W. *Vincent van Gogh*. Leipzig: Seeman, 1958.

GRUYTER. W. *De wereld van Van Gogh. Le Monde de Van Gogh. The World of Van Gogh*. Photography: Emmy Andrisse. The Hague: Daemen, 1953.

GUASTALLA, Pierre. *Essai sur Van Gogh*. Paris: Michel de Romilly, 1952.

HAMMACHER, Arno. *Van Gogh. The Land Where He Was Born and Raised. A Photographic Study*. The Hague: Boucher, 1953.

HAMMACHER, Arno. *Vincent van Gogh : Selbstbildnisse*. Stuttgart: Reclam, 1960.

HAMMACHER, Arno. *Genius and Disaster : The Ten Creative Years of Vincent van Gogh*. New York: Abrams, 1969.

HANSON, Lawrence and Elizabeth. *Portrait of Vincent, a Van Gogh Biography*. London: Chatto & Windus and Secker & Warburg, 1955. Published in the United States: *Passionate Pilgrim. The Life of Vincent van Gogh*. New York, 1955.

HARTLAUB, Gustav F. *Vincent van Gogh*. Berlin, Leipzig: Klinkhardt & Biermann, 1930.

HAUTECOEUR, Louis. *Van Gogh*. Monaco, Geneva: Documents d'art, 1946.

HAVELAAR, J. *Vincent van Gogh*. Netherlands, 1915. Zurich, 1920. Amsterdam, 1929, 1943.

HIND, C. Lewis. *Post-Impressionists*. London: Methuen, 1911.

HOLMER, F. *Van Gogh*. Stockholm, 1947.

HULSKER, Jan. *Wie war Vincent van Gogh*. The Hague: Bakker, 1958.

HULSKER, Jan. *Van Gogh's "Diary"*. New York: Morrow, 1971.

HULSKER, Jan. *Van Gogh door Van Gogh: De brieven als commentaar op zijn werk*. Amsterdam: Meulenhoff, 1973.

HUYGHE, René. *Vincent van Gogh*. Paris: Flammarion, 1958.

JAMES, Philip. *Van Gogh*. London: Faber & Faber, 1949.

JASPERS, Karl. *Strindberg und Van Gogh*. Berne, Leipzig: Bircher 1922. *Strindberg and Van Gogh*. Trans. by Oskar Crunow and David Woloslin. Tucson: University of Arizona Press, 1977.

KELLER, Horst. *Vincent van Gogh, Die Jahre der Vollendung*. Cologne, 1969. In English: *The Final Years*. New York: Abrams, 1969.

KNUTTEL, G. *Van Gogh der Holländer*. Stockholm, 1933.

KRAUS, G. *The Relationship Between Theo and Vincent van Gogh*. Amsterdam: Meulenhoff, 1954.

KUHN-FOELIX, August. *Vincent van Gogh, eine Psychographie*, Bergen, 1958

LA FAILLE, J.B. de. *L'Epoque française de Vincent van Gogh*. Paris: Bernheim-Jeune, 1927.

LA FAILLE, J.B. de. *Les faux Van Gogh*. Paris, Brussels: Van Oest, 1930.

LAPRADE, Jacques de. *Van Gogh*. Paris: Somogy, 1951.

LEPROCHON, Pierre. *Vincent van Gogh*. Cannes: Corymbe, 1972.

LEYMARIE, Jean. *Van Gogh*. Paris, New York: Tisné, 1951. New ed. New York: Rizzoli, 1977.

LEYMARIE, Jean. *Qui était Van Gogh?* Geneva: Skira, 1968.

LONGSTREET, Stephen. *The Drawings of Vincent van Gogh*. Los Angeles: Borden, 1963.

LOVGREN, S. *The Genesis of Modernism: Seurat, Gauguin, Van Gogh and French Symbolism in the 1880s*. Stockholm, 1959.

LUBIN, Albert. *Stranger on the Earth. A Psychological Biography of Vincent van Gogh*. New York: Holt, Rinehart & Winston, 1972.

LUZZATTO, G.L. *Vincent van Gogh*. Modena: Quanda, 1936.

MAROIS, Pierre. *Le Secret de Van Gogh*. Paris: Stock, 1957.

MAURON, C. *Van Gogh. Etudes psychocritiques*. Paris, 1976.

MEIER-GRAEFE, Julius. *Vincent van Gogh*. Munich: Piper, 1910, 1912, 1918, 1921, 1922, 1925. Trans. by John Holroyd Reece. London: Medici Society, 1922. New York, 1933.

MEIER-GRAEFE, Julius. *Vincent van Gogh*. 2 vol. Munich: Piper, 1921, 1925.

MEIER-GRAEFE, Julius. *Vincent van Gogh, der Zeichner*. Berlin: Otto Wecker, 1928.

METTRA, Claude. *L'Univers de Vincent van Gogh*. Paris: Scrépel, 1972. *Van Gogh's Universe*. Trans. by Nicole and Keith Gore. Woodbury, New York: Barron's, 1922.

MINKOWSKA, Françoise. *Van Gogh, sa maladie et son œuvre*. Paris: Presses du Temps présent, 1963.

MUENSTENBERGER, W. *Vincent van Gogh, Drawings, Pastels, Studies*. London: Falcon Press. Bussum, Netherland: Kroonder, 1947.

NAGERA, Humberto. *Vincent van Gogh: A Psychological Study*. New York: International University Press. London: George Allen & Unwin, 1967.

NIZON, Paul. *Die Anfänge Vincent van Goghs: der Zeichnungstil der holländischen Zeit. Untersuchung über die künstlerische Beziehung zur Psychologie und Weltanschauung des Künstlers*. Bern: Walter Fischer, 1960.

NORDENFALK, C. *Vincent van Gogh*. Stockholm, 1943. Copenhagen, 1946. Netherland and Norway, 1947. Engl. ed.: *The Life and Work of Van Gogh*. Trans. by Lawrence Wolfe. New York: Philosophical Library. London: Elek, 1953.

OUTHWAITE, D. *The Auvers Period of Vincent van Gogh*. Doctoral thesis, London University, 1969.

PACH, Walter. *Vincent van Gogh, 1853-1890. A Study of the Artist in Relation to His Time.* New York: Artbook Museum, 1936.

PARRONCHI, Alessandro. *Van Gogh.* Florence: Centro Italiano, 1944.

PERRUCHOT, Henri. *La Vie de Van Gogh.* Paris: Hachette, 1955.

PFISTER, Kurt. *Vincent van Gogh, sein Werk.* Potsdam: Kiepenheuer, 1922.

PIÉRARD, Louis. *La Vie tragique de Vincent van Gogh.* Paris: Crès, 1924, 1939. *The Tragic Life of Vincent van Gogh.* Trans. by Herbert Garland. London: Castle, 1925.

POLLOCK, G. and ORTON, F. *Vincent van Gogh, Artist of His Time.* Oxford: Phaidon. New York: Dutton, 1978.

REHORST, A.J. *De Hogeschoolrijdster, een onbekend werk van Vincent van Gogh.* Utrecht: De Banier, 1976.

REIDEMEISTER, L. *Auf den Spuren der Maler der Ile de France.* Berlin, 1963.

REWALD, J. *History of Impressionism.* 4th rev. ed. New York: Museum of Modern Art, 1980.

REWALD, J. *Post-Impressionism, from Van Gogh to Gauguin.* 3rd rev. ed. New York: Museum of Modern Art, 1978.

RIJKSMUSEUM KRÖLLER-MÜLLER. *A Detailed Catalogue with Full Documentation of 272 Works by Vincent van Gogh.* 4th ed. Otterlo, 1980.

ROËLANDT, Louis. *Vincent van Gogh et son frère Theo.* Paris: Flammarion, 1957.

ROSE, M. and MANNHEIM, M.J. *Vincent van Gogh im Spiegel seiner Handschrift.* Basel, Leipzig: Karger, 1938.

ROSKILL, Mark W. *Van Gogh, Gauguin and the Impressionist Circle.* Greenwich, Connecticut: New York Graphic Society, 1970.

ROSSET, A.M. *Van Gogh.* Paris: Tisné, 1941.

SCHERJON, W. *Catalogue des tableaux par Vincent van Gogh décrits dans ses lettres, Période Saint-Rémy et Auvers-sur-Oise.* Utrecht: Oosthoek, 1932.

SCHMIDT, G. *Vincent van Gogh. Leben und Werk.* Bern, 1947.

SECRÉTAN-ROLLIER, Pierre. *Van Gogh chez les gueules noires.* Lausanne: L'Age d'homme, 1977.

SHAPIRO, Meyer. *Vincent van Gogh.* New York: Abrams, 1957.

SHIBIKA, R. *La Vie de Vincent van Gogh et sa maladie mentale.* Tokyo, 1932.

STERNHEIM, Carl. *Gauguin und Van Gogh.* Berlin: Die Schmiede, 1924.

SZYMANSKA, Anna. *Unbekannte Jugendzeichnungen Vincent van Goghs.* East-Berlin: Henschelverlag, 1968.

TERRASSE, Charles. *Van Gogh.* Paris: Laurens, 1932; Floury, 1935.

TIETZE, Hans. *Vincent van Gogh.* Kunst in Holland No. 14. Vienna: Filser, 1922.

TRALBAUT, Marc Edo. *Vincent van Gogh in zijn Antwerpsche periode.* Amsterdam: Strengholt, 1948.

TRALBAUT, Marc Edo. *Vincent van Gogh en Charles de Groux.* Antwerp, 1953.

TRALBAUT, Marc Edo. *Vincent van Gogh te Antwerpen.* Antwerp, 1958.

TRALBAUT, Marc Edo. *Van Gogh: Eine Bildbiographie.* Munich: Kindler, 1958. In English: *Van Gogh: A Pictorial Biography.* Trans. by Margaret Shenfield. London: Thames & Hudson., New York: Viking, 1959.

TRALBAUT, Marc Edo. *Vincent van Gogh in Drenthe.* Aix-la-Chapelle: De Torenlaan, 1959.

TRALBAUT, Marc Edo. *Van Gogh.* Paris: Hachette, 1960.

TRALBAUT, Marc Edo. *Van Goghiana I-X.* Antwerp, 1963-1970.

TRALBAUT, Marc Edo. *Van Gogh, le mal aimé.* Lausanne, 1969.

TRALBAUT, Marc Edo. *Vincent van Gogh.* New York: Viking, 1969.

TREBLE, Rosemary. *Van Gogh and His Art.* New York: Galahad Books, 1975.

UEBERWASSER, W. *Le Jardin de Daubigny, das letzte Hauptwerk van Goghs.* Basel: Cratander, 1936.

VANBESELAERE, Walther. *De hollandsche periode (1880-1885) in het werk van Vincent van Gogh.* Amsterdam, Antwerp : De Sikkel, 1937.

VAN UITERT, Evert. *Vincent van Gogh. Zeichnungen.* Cologne: DuMont, 1977. *Van Gogh. Drawings.* Trans. by Elizabeth Willems Trieman. Woodstock, New York: Overlook Press, with Landshoff, Amsterdam, 1978.

VINCA, Masini I. *Van Gogh.* Florence, 1964.

VITALI, Lamberto. *Vincent van Gogh.* Milan: Hoepli, 1936.

WADLEY, Nicholas. *The Drawings of Vincent van Gogh.* Londres: Hamlyn, 1969.

WELSH-OVCHAROV, Bogomila M. *Van Gogh in Perspective.* Englewood Cliffs, New Jersey: Prentice Hall, 1974.

WELSH-OVCHAROV, Bogomila M. *Vincent van Gogh, His Paris Period, 1886-1888.* Utrecht and The Hague: Victorine, 1976.

WEISBACH, W. *Vincent van Gogh und Schicksal.* Basel: Amerbach, 1949, 1951.

WILM, Hubert. *Vincent van Gogh.* Munich: Hugendubel, 1935.

ZEMEL, Carol. *The Formation of a Legend: Van Gogh Criticism, 1890-1920.* Ann Arbor, Michigan: UMI Research Press, 1977.

MAJOR EXHIBITIONS

1966 *Vincent van Gogh. Paintings, watercolors and drawings.* Stedelijk Museum, Amsterdam.

1967-1968 *Van Gogh.* Dallas Museum of Art; Philadelphia Museum of Art; Toledo Museum of Art, Ohio; Art Gallery of Canada, Ottawa.

1969-1970 *Vincent van Gogh.* Los Angeles County Museum of Art; City Art Museum, Saint Louis; Philadelphia Museum of Art; Columbus Gallery of Fine Arts, Ohio.

1970 *Vincent van Gogh.* Kunstverein, Frankfurt.

1970-1971 *Vincent van Gogh.* Baltimore Museum of Art; De Young Museum of Fine Arts, San Francisco; Brooklyn Museum of Art, New York.

1972 *Vincent van Gogh.* Musée de l'Orangerie, Paris.

1972-1973 *Vincent van Gogh.* Musée des Beaux-Arts, Bordeaux; Kunstverein, Berne.

1974 *Van Gogh as Critic and Self-Critic.* Metropolitan Museum of Art, New York.
English Influences on Vincent van Gogh. University Art Gallery, Nottingham, Grande-Bretagne. Cat. de R. Pickvance.

1977 *Autobiographie de Vincent van Gogh à travers ses dessins et ses lettres.* Société du Salon d'automne, Paris.

1978 *Japanese Prints Collected by Vincent van Gogh.* Rijksmuseum Vincent van Gogh, Amsterdam. Int. by W. van Gulik, text by F. Orton.

1979 *Vincent van Gogh.* Odakyu Grand Gallery, Tokyo.

1980 *Van Gogh en Belgique.* Musée des Beaux-Arts, Mons.

Vincent van Gogh, The Influences of Nineteenth Century Illustrations. Florida State University, Tallahassee.

1980-1981 *Vincent van Gogh in zijn Hollandsche jaren.* Rijksmuseum, Amsterdam.

1981 *Vincent van Gogh and the Birth of Cloisonism.* Art Gallery of Ontario, Toronto. Cat. by B. Welsh-Ovcharov.

1984 *Van Gogh in Arles.* The Metropolitan Museum of Art, New York. Cat. by R. Pickvance.

1986-1987 *Van Gogh in Saint-Rémy and Auvers.* The Metropolitan Museum of Art. Cat. by R. Pickvance.

1988 *Van Gogh à Paris.* Musée d'Orsay, Paris.

ILLUSTRATIONS